MW01098643

Land of Liberty

# Virginia

by Judy Lloyd Anderson

**Consultant:**
Debbie Lou Tucker Hague
President, Social Studies Teacher
Virginia Council for
the Social Studies

Capstone *press*

Mankato, Minnesota

Capstone Press
151 Good Counsel Drive • P.O. Box 669 • Mankato, Minnesota 56002
http://www.capstone-press.com

*Library of Congress Cataloging-in-Publication Data*
Anderson, Judy Lloyd.
    Virginia / by Judy Lloyd Anderson.
        v. cm.—(Land of liberty)
    Includes bibliographical references (p. 61) and index.
    Contents: About Virginia—Land, climate, and wildlife—History of Virginia—
Government and politics—Economy and resources—People and culture—Virginia
cities—Virginia's land features—Peanut brittle—Virginia's flag and seal.
    ISBN 0-7368-2202-X (hardcover)
    1. Virginia—Juvenile literature. [1. Virginia.] I. Title. II. Series.
F226.3.A53 2004
975.5—dc21                                                          2002155470

Summary: An introduction to the geography, history, government, politics,
    economy, resources, people, and culture of Virginia, including maps, charts,
    and a recipe.

**Editorial Credits**
Christopher Harbo, editor; Jennifer Schonborn, series designer; Molly Nei, book
    designer; Enoch Peterson, illustrator; Kelly Garvin, photo researcher; Eric
    Kudalis, product planning editor

**Photo Credits**
Cover images: Monticello, Pat & Chuck Blackley; Blue Ridge Mountains, Digital
    Stock

Ann & Rob Simpson, 12–13; Ann & Rob Simpson/Gary W. Sargent, 16; Capstone
Press/Gary Sundermeyer, 54; Corbis, 26; Corbis/Bettmann, 29; Corbis/Buddy Mays,
42; Corbis/Tim Wright, 38; Cortez Austin Jr./GeoIMAGERY, 30–31; Courtesy of the
Chesapeake Bay Bridge-Tunnel, 17; Digital Stock, 1; Getty Images/Hulton Archive, 37;
Houserstock/Christie Parker, 4; Index Stock Imagery/Jeff Greenberg, 8; Index Stock
Imagery/Jim Schwabel, 52–53; Kent & Donna Dannen, 57; North Wind Picture
Archives, 18, 21, 24, 27; One Mile Up Inc., 55 (both); Pat & Chuck Blackley, 14, 32,
46, 49, 50, 63; Photo by Carol Diehl, 36; PhotoDisc Inc., 56; Robertstock/L. Smith,
43; Stock Montage Inc., 23, 58; U.S. Postal Service, 59; W. Lynn Seldon, Jr. 40–41, 45

**Artistic Effects**
Corbis, Corel, Digital Stock, PhotoDisc Inc., PhotoSpin

1 2 3 4 5 6 08 07 06 05 04 03

# Table of Contents

Thousands of white gravestones cover the rolling hills of Arlington National Cemetery.

# Chapter 1

# About Virginia

In 1864, former slave James Parks dug the first graves for Union soldiers at Arlington National Cemetery. As the Civil War (1861–1865) ended, thousands of Union soldiers were buried on land owned by Confederate General Robert E. Lee. Later, Confederate soldiers were buried there as well. Today, more than 260,000 military men, women, and their families rest beneath Arlington's white headstones.

Arlington National Cemetery has many monuments and memorials. They honor presidents, explorers, astronauts, and other national heroes. An "eternal flame" burns over the grave of President John F. Kennedy. The Challenger Space Shuttle

Memorial honors the seven astronauts who died onboard the shuttle in 1986.

Many services and ceremonies take place at the cemetery. Every day, visitors watch the changing of the guard at the Tomb of the Unknown Soldier. The tomb honors all unidentified U.S. soldiers killed in war. Soldiers guard the tomb 24 hours a day.

## The Mother of States

People often call Virginia the Mother of States. In 1584, Virginia's territory included all or part of eight future states. Minnesota, Wisconsin, Michigan, Illinois, Indiana, Ohio, West Virginia, and Kentucky were all part of Virginia.

Old Dominion is Virginia's official nickname. In the 1620s, King Charles I of England called Virginia his "old dominion" because people there were loyal to him.

Virginia is the 35th largest state. It covers 42,769 square miles (110,772 square kilometers). Washington, D.C., and

# Virginia Cities

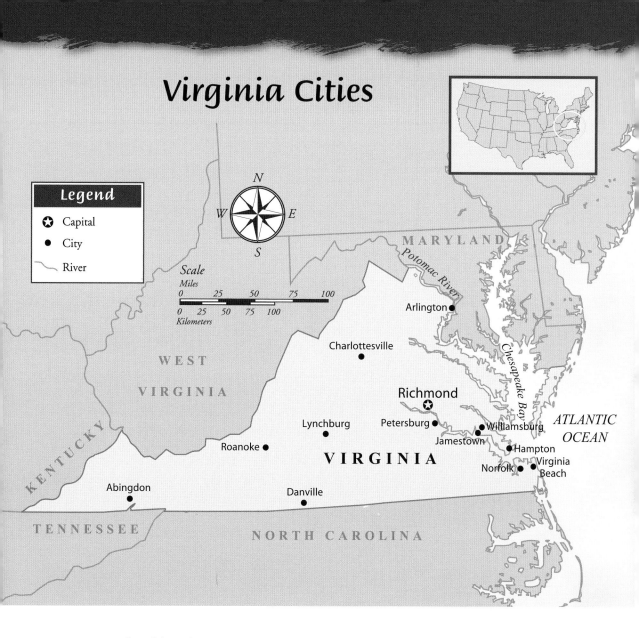

**Legend**
- ⊛ Capital
- ● City
- ⌇ River

Scale
Miles
0  25  50  75  100
0  25  50  75  100
Kilometers

MARYLAND

Potomac River

Chesapeake Bay

WEST
VIRGINIA

KENTUCKY

TENNESSEE

NORTH CAROLINA

ATLANTIC
OCEAN

Arlington ●

Charlottesville
●

Richmond ⊛

Lynchburg ●    Petersburg ●    ● Williamsburg

Roanoke ●                  Jamestown ●    ● Hampton

Abingdon ●        Danville ●        Norfolk ●  ● Virginia Beach

**VIRGINIA**

Maryland border Virginia on the northeast. The Atlantic
Ocean and Chesapeake Bay line Virginia's east coast.
Tennessee and North Carolina share Virginia's southern
border. West Virginia and Kentucky lie to the northwest.

Bridges over the Potomac River connect Virginia to Washington, D.C.

# Chapter 2

# Land, Climate, and Wildlife

Virginia's land is a mix of mountains, valleys, plateaus, and plains. The state has five main regions. These regions include the Coastal Plain, Piedmont Plateau, Blue Ridge, Ridge and Valley, and Appalachian Plateau.

## Coastal Plain

Virginia's Coastal Plain is also called the Tidewater Region. Peninsulas, called "necks" by Virginians, form the eastern edge of the region. The Northern Neck juts between the Potomac and Rappahannock Rivers. The Middle Neck lies between the Rappahannock and York Rivers. The Williamsburg Peninsula,

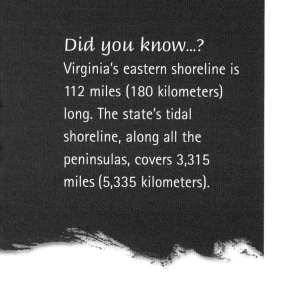
or the Southern Neck, is between the York and James Rivers.

Virginia's largest peninsula is the Eastern Shore. The Eastern Shore is part of the Delmarva Peninsula. It stretches into Chesapeake Bay and the Atlantic Ocean.

Farmland, marshes, and swamps make up much of the Coastal Plain. The Great Dismal Swamp lies in southern Virginia and northern North Carolina. At its center is Lake Drummond, the state's largest natural lake. The lake covers 3,142 acres (1,272 hectares).

The Coastal Plain ends at a natural border called the Fall Line. Along the Fall Line, a long ridge of granite runs north and south. Waterfalls and rapids flow over the ridge into the Coastal Plain.

## Piedmont Plateau

Virginia's largest region is the Piedmont Plateau. The term Piedmont means "land at the foot of the mountains." The plateau covers most of central Virginia from the Fall Line to the Blue Ridge Mountains. The land in the Piedmont rises

# Virginia's Land Features

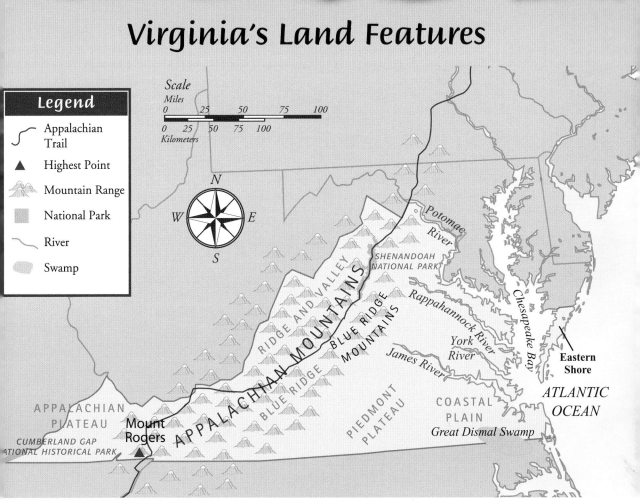

**Legend**

- Appalachian Trail
- ▲ Highest Point
- Mountain Range
- National Park
- River
- Swamp

Scale
Miles
0    25    50    75    100
0  25  50  75  100
Kilometers

N
W    E
S

APPALACHIAN PLATEAU
CUMBERLAND GAP NATIONAL HISTORICAL PARK
Mount Rogers ▲
RIDGE AND VALLEY
APPALACHIAN MOUNTAINS
BLUE RIDGE MOUNTAINS
BLUE RIDGE
SHENANDOAH NATIONAL PARK
Potomac River
Rappahannock River
York River
James River
PIEDMONT PLATEAU
COASTAL PLAIN
Great Dismal Swamp
Chesapeake Bay
Eastern Shore
ATLANTIC OCEAN

from 300 feet (90 meters) in the east to 2,000 feet (600 meters) in the west.

Many rivers cross the Piedmont and flow into the Coastal Plain. The James River is the longest. It runs 340 miles (547 kilometers) from the western Piedmont to Chesapeake Bay.

## Blue Ridge

The Blue Ridge region crosses Virginia from the north to the southwest. The Blue Ridge Mountains average 3,000 feet (900 meters) high in the north. In the south, their average height is about 4,000 feet (1,200 meters). Mount Rogers is the state's highest peak at 5,729 feet (1,746 meters).

People often vacation in the Blue Ridge Mountains. Shenandoah National Park lies in the region. Part of the Appalachian Trail runs through the park. This hiking path winds through 14 states from Georgia to Maine.

Luray Caverns are also in the Blue Ridge Mountains. Visitors can see caves full of colorful mineral formations.

## Ridge and Valley

Virginia's Ridge and Valley lies west of the Blue Ridge Mountains. This area is sometimes called the Great Valley. It includes many small ridges and valleys. The Shenandoah River flows south through the region.

The Shenandoah Valley lies in the Ridge and Valley region. The Massanutten Mountain ridge runs through much of the

Visitors to Shenandoah National Park can hike about 100 miles (161 kilometers) of the Appalachian Trail.

Shenandoah Valley. The Natural Bridge is in the southern end of the valley near Lexington. This bridge of rock stands 215 feet (66 meters) high and is 90 feet (27 meters) long. The Monacan Indians called it the Bridge of the Gods.

People can walk under the towering arch of the Natural Bridge. Scientists believe the rock bridge is more than 100 million years old.

## Appalachian Plateau

Virginia's Appalachian Plateau is also called the Cumberland Plateau. This flat, high land rises 2,000 to 3,000 feet (600 to 900 meters) above sea level. The Appalachian Plateau has mountains, streams, forests, and coal deposits.

Cumberland Gap National Historical Park is the most famous landmark in the region. In 1775, explorer Daniel Boone and others built the Wilderness Road. The road cut through a lower area in the mountains. The Wilderness Road made it easier for pioneers to travel through the mountains and settle in Kentucky.

## Climate

Virginia has a mild, humid coastal climate. The average summer temperature is 73 degrees Fahrenheit (23 degrees Celsius). Summer temperatures may climb to 100 degrees Fahrenheit (38 degrees Celsius) along the coast. Winter temperatures usually stay above freezing, but temperatures in the mountains can drop to minus 30 degrees Fahrenheit (minus 34 degrees Celsius).

With the Atlantic Ocean nearby, Virginia's air is usually moist. Humidity is higher and temperatures are warmer along the coast than in the mountains and valleys. The state receives about 42 inches (107 centimeters) of precipitation each year.

## Plants and Animals

Trees cover more than 60 percent of Virginia. Oak, pine, tupelo, cypress, and many other trees grow throughout the state. The blooming American dogwood is the state tree and flower.

Black bears climb the trees in Shenandoah National Park.

# Chesapeake Bay Bridge–Tunnel

People can drive their cars over and under the ocean to cross Chesapeake Bay. The Chesapeake Bay Bridge-Tunnel is 17.6 miles (28.3 kilometers) long. Since 1964, it has connected Virginia's mainland with the Eastern Shore.

The Chesapeake Bay Bridge-Tunnel is a series of bridges and two 1-mile (1.6-kilometer) underwater tunnels. When the roadway was planned, the U.S. Navy did not want a bridge to block their ship traffic in the bay. The ships can pass over the tunnels on their way to Norfolk Naval Base.

Virginia is also home to many animals. White-tailed deer, elk, black bears, bobcats, and mink live in the forests and mountains. More than 200 types of birds live in the state. The cardinal is Virginia's state bird. More than 80 types of snakes live in the state. Sea turtles, dolphins, and whales swim near Virginia's coast.

In the late 1600s, artist John White drew pictures of American Indians fishing and hunting in the Virginia area.

# Chapter 3

# History of Virginia

American Indians lived in Virginia long before Europeans arrived. The Powhatan grew corn, beans, pumpkins, melons, and tobacco along the Atlantic coast. The Monacan and Manahoac hunted bison in the Ridge and Valley region. The Susquehanna farmed and hunted in the Chesapeake Bay area. The Cherokee lived in the mountains. They also farmed and hunted.

In the 1500s, European fishers and treasure hunters explored the North American coast. In 1584, English explorer Sir Walter Raleigh claimed land along the Atlantic coast for England. He called the land Virginia to honor Queen Elizabeth I. She was known as the "Virgin Queen."

## Colonial Beginnings

In 1606, King James I of England gave the Virginia Company of London the right to settle in Virginia. The company sent 104 men. They hoped to find gold, jewels, fur, and other goods to trade.

In 1607, the colonists landed at Cape Henry on Virginia's coast. They then sailed up the James River about 60 miles (97 kilometers). The colonists set up a camp on a peninsula along the James River. They named their colony Jamestown. The land was swampy, and the water was salty. Within a few months, more than half of the colonists died from bad water and diseases carried by mosquitoes.

John Smith took leadership of the settlement. He traded tools for food with the Powhatan Confederation. This group controlled the land the colonists had settled. The Powhatan taught the colonists how to plant corn and catch fish.

For five years, the Virginia Company brought colonists to Virginia. Many of them died. The colonists who lived didn't make much money. In 1612, John Rolfe helped make the colony more successful. He grew a new type of tobacco.

# Pocahontas

Pocahontas is one of Virginia's most famous American Indians. In 1607, John Smith was captured and brought to her village. According to Smith, Pocahontas saved his life by stopping her father from killing him.

Years later, Pocahontas was kidnapped by English sailors. While she was held, she met John Rolfe. She and Rolfe married in 1614. Their marriage brought peace between the Powhatan and the colonists for several years.

In 1616, Rolfe, Pocahontas, and their son Thomas sailed to England to promote Virginia tobacco. After seven months in England, Pocahontas became sick and died. She was buried in Gravesend, England, in 1617.

He mixed strong seeds from American Indian tobacco with mild seeds from South American tobacco. He sent his "Virginia" tobacco to England. Many people liked it and bought it. The colonists planted more tobacco.

*"Give me liberty or give me death!"*

*—Patrick Henry, Virginia lawyer, 1775*

Good tobacco crops brought more settlers to the area. The settlers claimed more Powhatan land. Disagreements over land increased. On March 22, 1622, the Powhatan attacked the colonists. They killed 350 people. Virginians fought many battles with the Powhatan. In 1644, the Powhatan signed a treaty that gave most of their land to the English.

By 1700, huge tobacco plantations covered the colony. Plantation owners needed more people to plant and harvest their crops. They brought slaves from Africa to the colony. In 1730, more than 30,000 African slaves worked in Virginia.

## Steps Toward Statehood

In the mid-1700s, England still controlled Virginia. In 1765, the British Parliament issued the Stamp Act. This act made colonists pay taxes on newspapers, tea, and other English goods. A Virginia lawyer named Patrick Henry spoke out against the taxes. The colonists sent letters of protest to the king, but he ignored them. The colonists wanted freedom from England.

In 1776, colonial leaders held the Continental Convention in Philadelphia, Pennsylvania. The colonists voted to fight for

In 1775, Patrick Henry, standing in the center, spoke out against British taxes at the Virginia Assembly.

independence from England. Virginian Thomas Jefferson wrote the Declaration of Independence. On July 4, 1776, the colonial leaders signed the declaration to become free states.

During the Revolutionary War (1775–1783), Virginia began taking its first steps toward statehood. In 1776, the Commonwealth of Virginia adopted the first constitution of a free American state. Patrick Henry was elected the first governor of Virginia.

The last major battle of the Revolutionary War was fought in Virginia. In September 1781, George Washington's troops and French sailors trapped British troops at Yorktown. After days of fighting, British General Charles Cornwallis surrendered on October 19. The war ended two years later.

In 1787, Virginian James Madison helped write the U.S. Constitution. On June 25, 1788, Virginia ratified the Constitution and became the 10th state.

A farmer captured Nat Turner on October 31, 1831. Turner was later hanged for the slave revolt he led in Southampton.

## The Issue of Slavery

In the 1800s, slavery became a difficult issue in the United States. Plantation owners in the South wanted slaves to help them make a profit on their crops. Many people in the North believed slavery was wrong.

By the early 1800s, the United States had outlawed the capture and sale of slaves from Africa. But slaves already living in the country could still be bought and sold. Many slave families were broken up when slave owners sold children and parents to different plantations.

In August 1831, slave Nat Turner led a revolt in Southampton, Virginia. Turner was a slave who learned to read and had become a preacher. He and other slaves killed more than 50 whites before being caught and hanged.

## The Civil War

In 1860, Republican Abraham Lincoln was elected president. Lincoln and the Republican Party were against slavery. Eleven southern states voted to leave the Union. These states formed the Confederate States of America.

# Robert E. Lee

Robert E. Lee is a hero in Virginia. When the Civil War began, President Lincoln asked Lee to lead the Union army. Lee had a hard time deciding which side he should fight on. He wrote to his sister, "With all my devotion to the Union . . . I have not been able to make up my mind to raise my hand against my relatives, my children, my home."

Lee decided to fight with the Confederate army. In 1862, Confederate President Jefferson Davis gave Lee command of the Confederate army. Lee won many battles, but was forced to surrender in 1865.

After the war, Lee tried to bring the North and South together. He was the president of Washington College at Lexington until his death in 1870. The college is now called Washington and Lee University.

At first, Virginia tried not to take a side. When the Civil War began, President Lincoln called for troops to join the war. Virginia voted to join the other 10 Confederate states. Richmond, Virginia eventually became the Confederate capital.

Not everyone in Virginia was happy with the break from the Union. Leaders in western Virginia disagreed with the decision. In 1863, West Virginia broke away from Virginia. It became a state and joined the Union.

About half the Civil War's battles were fought in Virginia. Many battles took place in the Shenandoah Valley. The South won many of the first battles, but the Union won the war. On April 2, 1865, Union troops burned Richmond. Seven days later, Confederate General Robert E. Lee surrendered to Union General Ulysses S. Grant at Appomattox Courthouse.

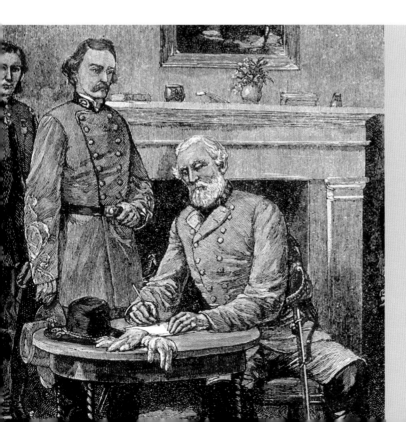

Confederate General Robert E. Lee, seated, surrendered to the Union army on April 9, 1865.

*Did you know...?*

Virginia has a state boat. The Chesapeake Bay deadrise was first used by Virginia fishers in the 1920s to catch oysters, clams, crabs, and fish. The deadrise became the state boat in 1988.

## Reconstruction

After the Civil War, Reconstruction (1865–1877) began in the South. Railroads, buildings, plantations, and homes needed to be rebuilt. Under military rule, new laws forced Virginia to give African Americans equal rights. Thousands of freed slaves needed food and places to live. Many African Americans moved out of the state. In 1870, Virginia rejoined the Union.

After Reconstruction, Virginia's economy began to improve. People built cigarette factories, textile mills, railroads, coal mines, and shipbuilding plants in the state.

## Growth and Development

Virginia's economy continued to improve in the early 1900s. In 1917, President Woodrow Wilson sent U.S. troops to fight in World War I (1914–1918). Many military training centers and new factories were built in Virginia.

In the 1930s, the Great Depression (1929–1939) put people throughout the United States out of work. President Franklin D. Roosevelt created jobs for people to build parks,

In 1933, President Franklin D. Roosevelt, seated at the head of the table, visited Civilian Conservation Corps camps in the Shenandoah Valley.

roads, and buildings. Thousands of young men joined the Civilian Conservation Corps to help build Shenandoah National Park.

World War II (1939–1945) helped end the Great Depression. Thousands of soldiers came to Virginia's military bases. After the war, many military and government workers stayed in Virginia.

## Segregation

Equal rights for African Americans came slowly in Virginia. In the early 1900s, Virginia passed segregation laws to separate African Americans from whites in public places.

In 1954, the U.S. Supreme Court ruled that segregation in public schools was against the law. Virginia passed laws in protest. These laws allowed schools to close instead of integrate. Prince Edward County closed its public schools from 1959 to 1965. Virginia did not pass laws to integrate its schools until 1969.

## Recent Years

In recent years, the growth in the number of government jobs has made Virginia's economy strong. Thousands of Virginians work at the Norfolk Naval Base, the Central Intelligence Agency (CIA) Headquarters, and the Pentagon. The Pentagon is the headquarters for the United States Department of Defense.

On September 11, 2001, the Pentagon was a target of terrorist attacks. Highjackers took over an American airliner and crashed it into the Pentagon. The crash killed 189 people and damaged one section of the building.

Terrorists crashed an American Airlines 757 airliner into Wedge 1 of the Pentagon on September 11, 2001. Fire damaged much of the area around the crash site.

Thomas Jefferson designed the center building of Virginia's state capitol.

# Chapter 4

# Government and Politics

Virginia was formed as a commonwealth. This form of government gives the people the right to make laws. Virginia has the oldest representative government in the United States. The first law-making body, the House of Burgesses, met July 30, 1619. A burgess was a person elected to represent a region of the state. Today, Virginia's government has executive, legislative, and judicial branches.

## Branches of Government

Virginia's governor leads the executive branch. A lieutenant governor and an attorney general serve under the governor. The governor appoints the state treasurer and other executive

officers. The governor signs or vetoes bills passed by the legislative branch.

Virginia's legislative branch is called the general assembly. The general assembly has a senate and a house of delegates. Virginia's general assembly has 40 senators and 100 delegates. Assembly members make and change laws. They also decide how much to tax citizens and how money should be spent.

The Virginia Supreme Court is the highest court in the state's judicial branch. The supreme court has seven justices who are each elected to 12-year terms. The court explains laws made by the legislature. It also hears cases brought from the court of appeals. The court of appeals hears cases appealed from the state's lower courts. The lower courts include circuit courts, general district courts, and juvenile and domestic relations courts.

Virginia's local government is divided into counties and independent cities. Virginia has 95 counties. The state also has 40 independent cities. These cities do not belong to specific counties.

# Virginia's State Government

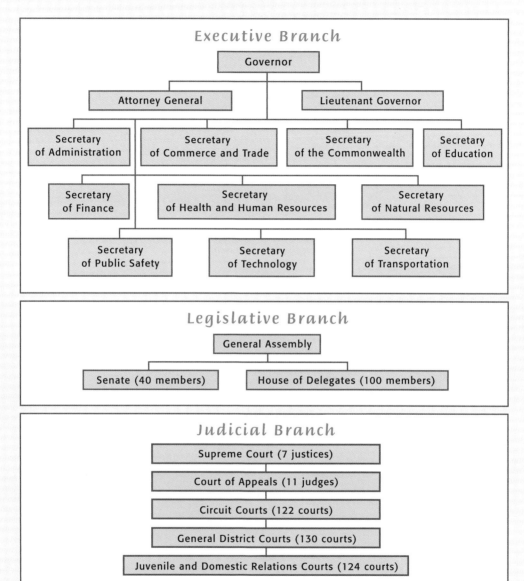

**Executive Branch**

Governor

Attorney General | Lieutenant Governor

Secretary of Administration | Secretary of Commerce and Trade | Secretary of the Commonwealth | Secretary of Education

Secretary of Finance | Secretary of Health and Human Resources | Secretary of Natural Resources

Secretary of Public Safety | Secretary of Technology | Secretary of Transportation

**Legislative Branch**

General Assembly

Senate (40 members) | House of Delegates (100 members)

**Judicial Branch**

Supreme Court (7 justices)

Court of Appeals (11 judges)

Circuit Courts (122 courts)

General District Courts (130 courts)

Juvenile and Domestic Relations Courts (124 courts)

## Mother of Presidents

People call Virginia the "Mother of Presidents" because eight U.S. presidents have come from the state. George Washington, Thomas Jefferson, James Madison, and James Monroe served as four of the first five U.S. presidents. Virginians John Tyler, William Henry Harrison, Zachary Taylor, and Woodrow Wilson were also presidents.

People can tour the mansion and grounds of George Washington's Mount Vernon estate.

# Lawrence Douglas Wilder

Lawrence Douglas Wilder grew up in Richmond, Virginia. He went to segregated public schools in Richmond. He later earned a degree in chemistry from Virginia Union University.

In the 1950s, Wilder joined the army. He earned a Bronze Star for heroism during the Korean War (1950–1953). After the war, he earned a law degree from Howard University in Washington, D.C.

In 1969, Wilder entered politics. He became the first African American elected to the state senate since Reconstruction. In 1985, he was elected lieutenant governor. In 1989, Wilder became the first African American elected governor in the United States. He was Virginia's governor from 1990 to 1994.

Today, the Virginia homes and birthplaces of many of these presidents are open to visitors. Many people travel to Virginia to learn more about the state's role in the birth of the nation. Visitors can tour Jefferson's Monticello home in Charlottesville and Washington's Mount Vernon home near Alexandria.

U.S. sailors and marines often
return to the Norfolk Naval Base
after their tour of duty at sea.

# Economy and Resources

In colonial times, Virginia's economy relied on tobacco. Today, the state depends on more than agriculture. Virginia is a leader in the service and technology industries. The state also produces many important manufactured goods and natural resources.

## Service Industries

Service industries make up the largest part of Virginia's economy. The state's key service industries include government, military, media, and tourism. Together, they make up more than two-thirds of the state's economy.

The federal government is Virginia's largest employer. More than 20,000 people work at the Pentagon. Thousands of people also work at Langley Air Force Base and NASA's Langley Research Center in Hampton. The CIA has its headquarters in Langley. The Norfolk Naval Base and the Quantico Marine Corps Base train many of the country's military members.

The media has been an important industry for the state since colonial times. In 1736, the colony started its first

newspaper called the *Virginia Gazette*. Today, Virginia produces more than 200 newspapers and more than 400 magazines. *USA Today* is one of 100 papers published by the Gannett Company of Arlington.

Tourism is another large part of Virginia's economy. Tourists spend more than $11 billion in the state each year. Millions of people visit the state's monuments, national parks, historic museums, and theme parks. Virginia Beach, the state's largest city, draws tourists from across the country

Tourists can ride horse-drawn carriages through the streets of Colonial Williamsburg.

# Virginia Air and Space Center

In 1992, the Virginia Air and Space Center opened in Hampton. It serves as the visitor center for NASA's Langley Research Center. The museum is made of glass, steel, and brick. It looks like a bird in flight.

Visitors to the center can learn about the first astronauts and the equipment NASA used. Several early airplanes hang from the ceiling. The *Apollo 12* spacecraft, a space suit, Moon rocks, and other objects from space flights fill the building. Visitors can watch movies about space exploration in a five-story IMAX theater.

to its sandy beaches. Jamestown and Colonial Williamsburg show visitors what life was like in the 1700s. The Museum of the Confederacy in Richmond teaches visitors about the state's Civil War history. In western Virginia, people visit the Cumberland Gap National Historical Park.

## Transportation and Manufacturing

Shipbuilding was one of Virginia's earliest industries. The Gosport Shipyard was built in 1767. Shipbuilding and repair is still a leading industry in Norfolk, Newport News, and Portsmouth. Newport News Shipbuilding is one of the largest shipbuilders in the world. The company builds aircraft carriers and submarines.

Railroads are also important to the state. Virginia's CSX and Norfolk Southern are two of the largest railroad companies in the United States. Both railroads carry Virginia's products to other states around the country.

Virginia manufactures many items. Soft drinks, beer, and tobacco products are its leading manufactured products.

Newport News Shipbuilding uses large cranes to build ships.

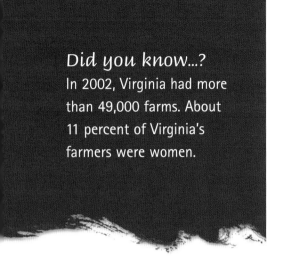

Chemicals and transportation equipment, such as trucks and motor parts, rank next. The state also produces food products, paper products, computer equipment, and tires.

## Agriculture

Agriculture is an important part of Virginia's economy. Poultry, cattle, hogs, and other livestock bring in most of the state's farm income. Tobacco is one of Virginia's largest crops. Universal Corporation in Richmond is one of the world's largest sellers of tobacco leaves. Virginia farmers also grow corn, soybeans, peanuts, potatoes, apples, and peaches.

## Natural Resources

Virginia's waters and forests are important natural resources for the state's economy. Virginia is one of the top commercial fishing states. People catch oysters, scallops, and blue crab in Virginia waters. The state also harvests trees used for construction materials and paper.

Blue crabs get their name from their blue-colored legs. Virginia fishers harvest most of the state's blue crabs in Chesapeake Bay.

Mining is an important industry in Virginia. Coal mines produce more than 30 million tons (27 million metric tons) of coal each year. The state is also the largest producer of kyanite in the nation. This mineral is used to make bricks. Virginia gravel, sand, and rock is mainly used for concrete and construction projects.

Many Virginians enjoy the annual
Dogwood Festival parade in Charlottesville.

# Chapter 6

# People and Culture

Virginia has one of the fastest growing populations in the United States. In Virginia's early days, most of its people lived on farms. Now, government, military, and technology jobs bring people to the state's cities. Two-thirds of Virginia's people live in and around cities.

Virginia's mix of races has changed during its history. The population was once equally divided between whites, African Americans, and American Indians. Today, almost three-fourths of Virginians are white. African Americans make up about 20 percent of the state's population. American Indians make up less than one percent of the population. Recently, more Hispanic and Asian people have moved to the state.

# Virginia's Ethnic Background

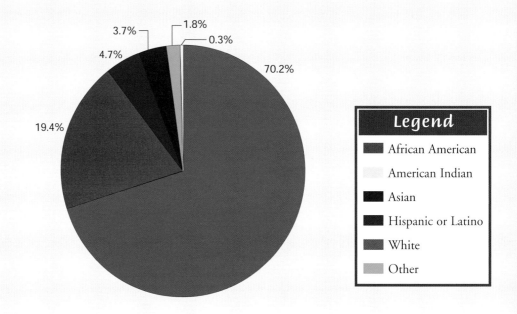

- 3.7%
- 1.8%
- 0.3%
- 4.7%
- 70.2%
- 19.4%

**Legend**
- African American
- American Indian
- Asian
- Hispanic or Latino
- White
- Other

## Education

Education has always been important in Virginia. In 1634, the Virginia General Assembly opened Syms School in Hampton. It was the first free school in the colonies. Private schools, called old field schools, were built in the 1700s for elementary students. In 1779, Thomas Jefferson wanted the state to pay for elementary education. Almost 100 years later, the state began paying for public schools.

Virginia has a history of providing people quality higher education. In 1693, the College of William and Mary began teaching boys at Williamsburg. In 1819, Thomas Jefferson started the University of Virginia at Charlottesville. Today, the state has 39 public and 50 private colleges and universities.

## Historical Attractions

History is still a big part of Virginia's charm. Eastern Virginia is the center of colonial history. Millions of tourists visit Williamsburg, Jamestown, and Yorktown. The area is called "The Historic Triangle." Colonial Williamsburg looks much

Thomas Jefferson designed the Rotunda at the University of Virginia at Charlottesville.

People reenact the Civil War's Battle of New Market in Virginia's Shenandoah Valley. The real battle took place on May 15, 1864.

like it did at the time of the Revolutionary War. Workers at Colonial Williamsburg dress and perform similar to people who lived in the 1700s.

Many tourists come to the state to see Civil War museums and battlefields. At the Mariner's Museum in Newport News, visitors learn about the Civil War battle between the U.S.S.

*Monitor* and the C.S.S. *Virginia*. Tourists also visit Manassas, Fredericksburg, Petersburg, and other Civil War battlefields throughout the state.

## Art, Music, and Food

Art is important to Virginians. Museums show American Indian artifacts at Jamestown. Hampton and Williamsburg have museums with African American art and folk art. Artists also show their art at shops, festivals, and shows. The Boardwalk Art Festival in Virginia Beach and the Virginia Highlands Festival in Abingdon are held each summer.

Virginia also has a rich music history. Jazz singers Pearl Bailey and Ella Fitzgerald were born in Newport News. Country singer Patsy Cline started her career in Winchester. The Statler Brothers began singing country music in Staunton.

Southern cooking is famous in Virginia. Many old recipes are from colonial times. Favorite dishes include Virginia ham, sweet-potato pie, peanut soup, oyster stew, crab cakes, and pecan pie.

## Sports

Virginia has no professional sports teams. Many people follow college basketball and football teams. Golf is also a favorite activity. The state has many golf courses. The Tournament Players Club of Virginia Beach and Kingsmill in Williamsburg have held PGA and LPGA tournaments.

Horses are a big part of Virginia's sports culture. Horse races and steeplechases are held throughout the summer. Foxhunts with horses and hunting dogs are also held in the state.

Auto racing is popular in Virginia. Stock car races are held in Richmond and Martinsville. The Richmond International Raceway and the Martinsville Speedway are the state's two NASCAR tracks.

Virginia's rich history and southern culture welcomes millions of people to the state each year. From Jamestown to Arlington National Cemetery, the Mother of States shows visitors how one state helped shape the history of an entire nation.

Every year, Martinsville Speedway hosts the Virginia 500 and the Old Dominion 500 as part of NASCAR's Winston Cup series.

# Recipe: Peanut Brittle

*Peanuts are one of Virginia's main crops. Peanuts are often used in soups and desserts. Peanut brittle is easy to make in the microwave.*

## Ingredients

1 ½ cups (360 mL) unsalted
    peanuts
1 cup (240 mL) sugar
½ cup (120 mL) light corn syrup
1 teaspoon (5 mL) butter
1 teaspoon (5 mL) vanilla
1 teaspoon (5 mL) baking soda

## Equipment

nonstick cooking spray
baking sheet
large microwavable bowl
dry-ingredient measuring
    cups
liquid measuring cup
mixing spoon
pot holders
measuring spoons
table knife

## What You Do

1. Spray baking sheet with nonstick cooking spray. Set aside.

2. In large microwavable bowl, stir together peanuts, sugar, and corn syrup.

3. Microwave on high 4 minutes. Using pot holders, remove bowl from microwave and stir mixture with mixing spoon.

4. Microwave on high 3 minutes.

5. Stir in butter and vanilla.

6. Microwave on high 1½ minutes.

7. Add baking soda. Quickly stir until mixture is light and foamy.

8. Immediately pour mixture onto prepared baking sheet. Spread mixture with table knife.

9. Cool. Break hardened candy into pieces.

Makes 15–20 pieces

# Virginia's Flag and Seal

## Virginia's Flag

Virginia's state flag was adopted in 1861. The flag is dark blue with a white circle in the center. The state seal of Virginia is inside the white circle.

## Virginia's State Seal

Virginia's state seal was adopted by the state's Constitutional Convention in 1776. The seal shows the Roman goddess Virtus standing above a defeated tyrant. Virtus holds a spear and a sword. The tyrant holds a broken chain. The state's motto, "Sic Semper Tyrannis," is printed near the bottom of the seal. It means "Thus Always to Tyrants."

# Almanac

General Facts

Nickname: Old Dominion State

Population: 7,078,515 (U.S. Census 2000)
Population rank: 12th

Capital: Richmond

Largest Cities: Virginia Beach, Norfolk, Chesapeake, Richmond, Newport News

Agriculture

Agricultural products: Poultry, beef cattle, corn, hogs, milk, peanuts, tobacco, soybeans, apples, cotton

Climate

Average summer temperature:
73 degrees Fahrenheit (23 degrees Celsius)

Average winter temperature:
37 degrees Fahrenheit (3 degrees Celsius)

Average annual precipitation: 42 inches (107 centimeters)

Area: 42,769 square miles (110,772 square kilometers)
Size rank: 35th

Highest point: Mount Rogers 5,729 feet (1,746 meters) above sea level

Lowest point: Atlantic coast, sea level

Geography

Cardinal

American foxhounds

Symbols

**Bird:** Cardinal

**Boat:** Chesapeake Bay deadrise

**Dance:** Square Dance

**Dog:** American foxhound

**Economy**

**Natural resources:** Trees, fish, coal, sand, gravel, kyanite, clay

**Types of industry:** Chemicals, tobacco products, food products, transportation equipment, tourism, fishing

**Symbols**

**Fish:** Brook trout

**Flower and tree:** American dogwood

**Insect:** Tiger swallowtail butterfly

**Shell:** Oyster

**Government**

**First governor:** Patrick Henry, 1776–1779

**Statehood:** June 25, 1788 (10th state)

**U.S. Representatives:** 11

**U.S. Senators:** 2

**U.S. electoral votes:** 13

**Counties:** 95

**Independent cities:** 40

# Timeline

**1607**
The Virginia Company builds the first British colony at Jamestown.

**1622**
The Powhatan Indians kill 350 Virginia colonists.

**1788**
Virginia becomes a state.

**1781**
The British surrender to George Washington at Yorktown.

**1831**
Nat Turner leads a slave revolt in Southampton.

**1865**
General Robert E. Lee surrenders the Confederate army to General Ulysses S. Grant at Appomattox Courthouse.

**1620**
Pilgrims establish Massachusetts Bay Colony.

**1775–1783**
American colonies fight for independence from Great Britain in the Revolutionary War.

**1812–1814**
The United States fights Great Britain in the War of 1812.

**1861–1865**
Union states fight Confederate states in the Civil War.

**1950s**

Virginia General Assembly passes laws to stop integration of public schools.

**1964**

The Chesapeake Bay Bridge–Tunnel is completed.

**2001**

Terrorists attack the Pentagon and the World Trade Center on September 11.

**1930s**

The Civilian Conservation Corps help build Shenandoah National Park.

**1989**

Lawrence Douglas Wilder becomes the first elected African American governor in the United States.

**1929–1939**

The United States experiences the Great Depression.

**1964**

U.S. Congress passes the Civil Rights Act, which makes discrimination illegal.

**1914–1918**

World War I is fought; the United States enters the war in 1917.

**1939–1945**

World War II is fought; the United States enters the war in 1941.

**1991**

The United States fights Iraq in the Gulf War.

# Words to Know

**commonwealth** (KOM-uhn-welth)—a type of government in which the people have a right to make laws

**Confederacy** (kuhn-FED-ur-uh-see)—the 11 southern states that left the United States to form the Confederate States of America

**constitution** (kon-stuh-TOO-shuhn)—an official document that explains the laws of a country

**dominion** (duh-MIN-yuhn)—a large area of land owned by a single ruler

**integrate** (IN-tuh-grate)—to bring people of different races together in schools and other public places

**peninsula** (puh-NIN-suh-luh)—a piece of land surrounded by water on three sides

**plantation** (plan-TAY-shuhn)—a large farm where one main crop is grown

**Reconstruction** (ree-kuhn-STRUHK-shuhn)—the period after the Civil War when the Southern states reorganized their governments

**segregation** (seg-ruh-GAY-shuhn)—the policy of separating people according to their race

# To Learn More

**Burgan, Michael.** *George Washington.* Profiles of the Presidents. Minneapolis: Compass Point Books, 2002.

**DeAngelis, Gina.** *Virginia.* From Sea to Shining Sea. New York: Children's Press, 2001.

**Monroe, Judy.** *Robert E. Lee.* Let Freedom Ring. Mankato, Minn.: Bridgestone Books, 2002.

**Young, Robert.** *A Personal Tour of Monticello.* How it Was. Minneapolis: Lerner Publications, 1999.

# Internet Sites

Do you want to find out more about Virginia?
Let FactHound, our fact-finding hound dog, do the research for you.

Here's how:
1) Visit ***http://www.facthound.com***
2) Type in the **Book ID** number:
   **073682202X**
3) Click on **FETCH IT**.

FactHound will fetch Internet sites picked by our editors just for you!

# Places to Write and Visit

**Arlington National Cemetery**
Arlington, VA  22211

**Luray Caverns**
970 U.S. Highway 221 West
P.O. Box 748
Luray, VA  22835

**The Museum of the Confederacy**
1201 East Clay Street
Richmond, VA  23219

**Virginia Air and Space Center**
600 Settlers Landing Road
Hampton, VA  23669

**Virginia Historical Society**
428 North Boulevard
Richmond, VA  23221-0311

A statue of Robert E. Lee is one of six statues along Monument Avenue in Richmond.